MLB's Greatest Teams

TEXAS RANGERS

Big Buddy Books
An Imprint of Abdo Publishing
abdopublishing.com

Katie Lajiness

abdopublishing.com

Published by Abdo Publishing, a division of ABDO, PO Box 398166, Minneapolis, Minnesota 55439.

Printed in the United States of America, North Mankato, Minnesota.
052018
092018

THIS BOOK CONTAINS RECYCLED MATERIALS

Cover Photo: Tom Pennington/Getty Images.
Interior Photos: 33ft/Depositphotos (p. 7); Bob Levey/Getty Images (p. 15); Brian Bahr/Getty Images (p. 23); Elsa/Getty Images (p. 17); Getty Images (p. 22); Jamie Squire/Getty Images (pp. 23, 25); Pool/Getty Images (p. 19); Rick Stewart/Getty Images (p. 22); Rick Yeatts/Getty Images (pp. 5, 29); Rob Tringali/Getty Images (p. 24); Ronald Martinez/Getty Images (pp. 9, 13, 28); Stephen Dunn/Getty Images (p. 21); Victor Decolongon/Getty Images (p. 27); The Washington Post/Getty Images (p. 11).

Coordinating Series Editor: Tamara L. Britton
Graphic Design: Jenny Christensen

Library of Congress Control Number: 2017962675

Publisher's Cataloging-in-Publication Data

Names: Lajiness, Katie, author.
Title: Texas Rangers / by Katie Lajiness.
Description: Minneapolis, Minnesota : Abdo Publishing, 2019. | Series: MLB's greatest teams | Includes online resources and index.
Identifiers: ISBN 9781532115219 (lib.bdg.) | ISBN 9781532155932 (ebook)
Subjects: LCSH: Major League Baseball (Organization)--Juvenile literature. | Baseball teams--United States--History--Juvenile literature. | Texas Rangers (Baseball team)--Juvenile literature. | Sports teams--Juvenile literature.
Classification: DDC 796.35764--dc23

Contents

Major League Baseball

League Play

There are two leagues in MLB. They are the American League (AL) and the National League (NL). Each league has 15 teams and is split into three divisions. They are east, central, and west.

The Texas Rangers is one of 30 Major League Baseball (MLB) teams. The team plays in the American League West **Division**.

Throughout the season, all MLB teams play 162 games. The season begins in April and can continue until November.

Captain has been the Rangers' mascot since 2002. This horse wears number 72 to honor the year the Rangers moved to Arlington, Texas.

A Winning Team

The Rangers team is from Arlington, Texas. The team's colors are red, blue, and white.

The team has had good seasons and bad. But time and again, the Rangers players have proven themselves. Let's see what makes the Rangers one of MLB's greatest teams!

Fast Facts

HOME FIELD: Globe Life Park

TEAM COLORS: Red, blue, and white

TEAM SONG: "I Like Texas" by Pat Green

PENNANTS: 2

WORLD SERIES TITLES: None

CANADA
UNITED STATES OF AMERICA
MEXICO
Oklahoma
New Mexico
Arkansas
Texas
Arlington
Louisiana
MEXICO
GULF OF MEXICO
N
W
E
S

Globe Life Park

In 1961, the team began playing at Griffith Stadium in Washington, DC. After one year, it moved to the Robert F. Kennedy Stadium until 1971. This new stadium could hold nearly 20,000 more people.

The Rangers moved to Arlington in 1972. First, the team played in the Arlington Stadium. Then in 1994, it moved to its current home at Globe Life Park. More than 48,000 fans can sit in the park!

The Rangers team plans to move out of Globe Life Park in 2020. But, it won't move far. The new stadium will be across the street from the old one.

Then and Now

Before it was the Rangers, the team was the Washington Senators. The Senators began playing in 1961. The team struggled on the field for many years. So, owner Bob Short moved the team to Arlington in 1972. He renamed the team the Texas Rangers after the famous police force.

In the 1970s and 1980s, the team did not make it to the **playoffs**. But, the players did place second in their **division** five times.

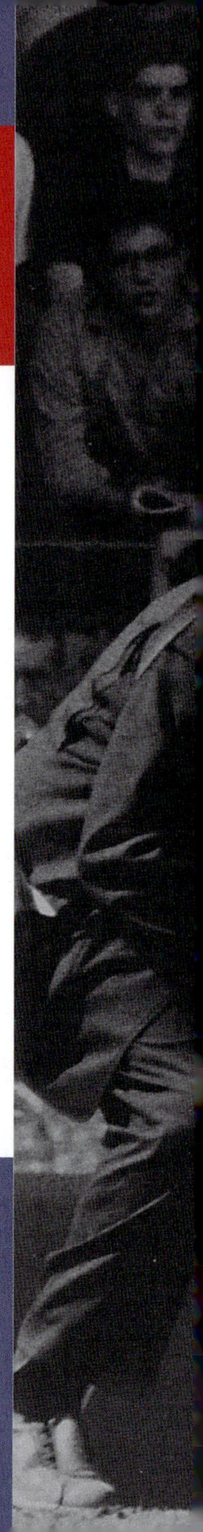

There were two different Senators teams in Washington, DC. One team moved to Minnesota and became the Twins. The other moved to Texas and became the Rangers.

By the mid-1990s, the Rangers had built a lineup of powerful hitters. Star players helped the Rangers win AL West titles in 1996, 1998, and 1999.

In the early 2000s, the team welcomed star player Alex Rodriguez. But he failed to help the team out of last place in its **division**. Then the team began rebuilding.

In 2010 and 2011, the Rangers won their first two **pennants** since moving to Texas. But, the team lost both World Series.

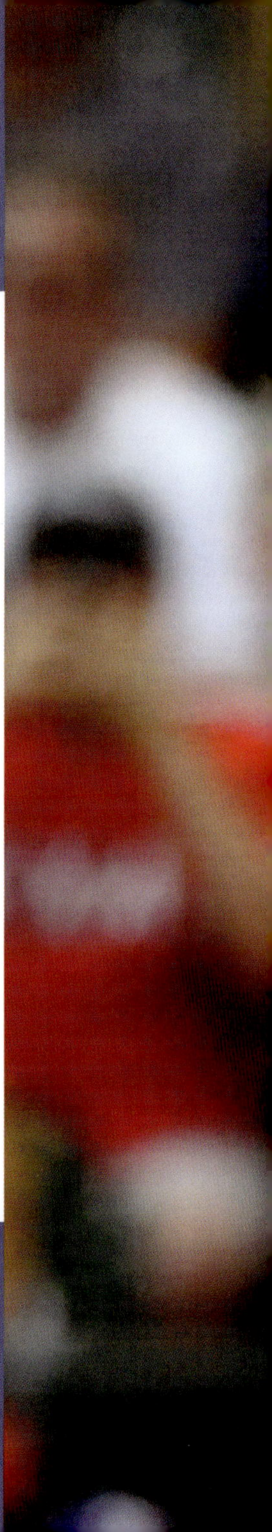

Throughout history, no major league player has hit five home runs in one game. But the Rangers' Josh Hamilton has hit four home runs in a game.

Highlights

For many years, the Rangers have fought to earn the biggest titles in baseball. With hard work, the team has made it into the **postseason** eight times. And twice it beat the Tampa Bay Rays to win its **division**.

The Rangers' two main rivals are the Houston Astros and the Toronto Blue Jays.

Win or Go Home

The top team from each AL and NL division goes to the playoffs. Each league also sends one wild-card team. One team from the AL and one from the NL will win the pennant. The two pennant winners then go to the World Series!

In 2010, the team beat the New York Yankees and moved on to the World Series. The next year, the Rangers beat the Detroit Tigers and went to their second World Series.

The Rangers have won two AL **pennants**. But the team is still waiting for a World Series title.

During the 2010 playoffs, the Rangers celebrated a 6–1 win over the Yankees.

Famous Managers

A former **professional** player, Ron Washington went on to work as a base coach. In 2007, Washington began managing the Texas Rangers. He took the team to the World Series in both 2010 and 2011. Washington managed the team until 2014.

Before he managed the Rangers, Washington played in MLB. He was an infielder for 10 years with five different teams.

Johnny Oates managed the Rangers from 1995 to 2001. In seven seasons, he led the team to 506 total wins. He managed four **Most Valuable Players (MVPs)** during his 11-year coaching **career**. In 1996, Oates earned the AL Manager of the Year Award.

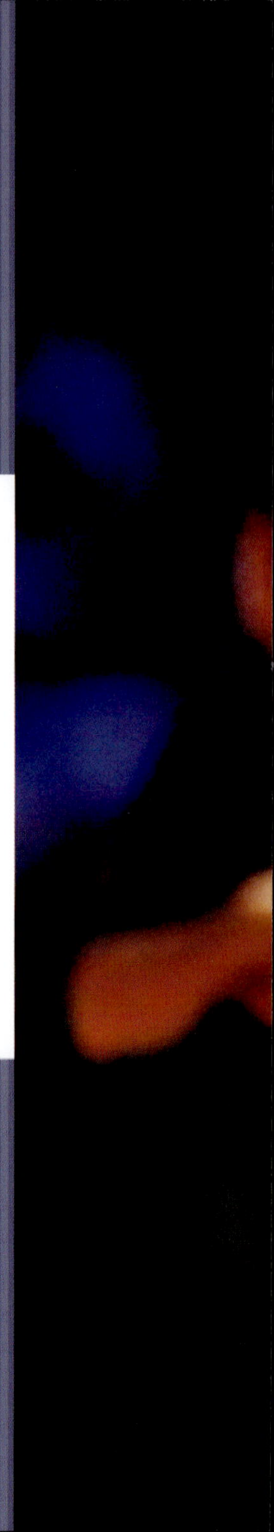

In 1996, Oates led the Rangers into the team's first postseason wins.

Star Players

Nolan Ryan PITCHER, #34

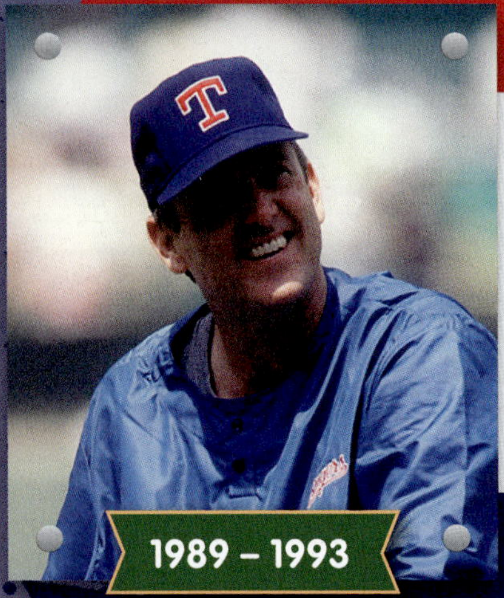

Many believe that Nolan Ryan was one of the best pitchers in MLB history. He was 42 years old when he joined the Rangers in 1989. Ryan finished his **career** having played in MLB for a record-tying 27 seasons. He joined the National Baseball Hall of Fame in 1999.

Iván Rodríguez CATCHER, #7

Iván "Pudge" Rodríguez played in ten All-Star Games during his time with the Rangers. This is the highest number for any catcher in history. In 1999, Rodríguez earned the AL **MVP** Award. He was **inducted** into the National Baseball Hall of Fame in 2017.

Alex Rodriguez SHORTSTOP, #3

During his three seasons with the Rangers, Alex Rodriguez led the AL in home runs. He earned the Hank Aaron Award for best hitter in the AL for 2002. He won two **Gold Glove Awards** in the short time he was with the Rangers. And in 2003, Rodriguez won his first **MVP** Award.

Michael Young THIRD BASEMAN, #10

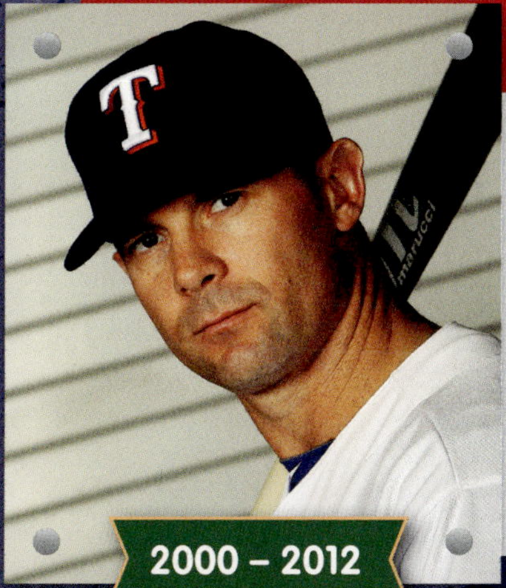

During his time with the Rangers, Michael Young took part in seven All-Star Games. In 2008, he won a Gold Glove Award. A star player, he was named the 2005 AL batting **champion**. Young was **inducted** into the Texas Rangers Hall of Fame in 2016.

Elvis Andrus SHORTSTOP, #1

At age 20, Elvis Andrus became the Rangers' starting shortstop. He took 33 stolen bases in his **rookie** season. In 2013, Andrus finished the year scoring 91 runs. A year later, he enjoyed a 39-game hitting streak, including eight homers. And in 2017, he hit a staggering 20 home runs for the Rangers.

Adrián Beltré THIRD BASEMAN, #29

As a Ranger, Adrián Beltré has taken part in three All-Star Games. He has earned three **Gold Glove** and two **Platinum Glove** awards while with the Rangers. With 199 hits in 2013, he earned the most hits in the AL for that year. And in 2014, he received the Lou Gehrig Memorial Award.

Nomar Mazara RIGHT FIELDER, #30

Nomar Mazara made a home run during his first MLB appearance. He also won the AL **Rookie** of the Month Award two months in a row. In 2017, Mazara hit 20 home runs and 97 **runs batted in (RBIs)**. This helped him earn the AL Player of the Week in April 2017.

Final Call

The Rangers have a long, rich history. The team has been to the **playoffs** eight times. And team members have played in two World Series.

Even during losing seasons, true fans have stuck by the team. Many believe the Rangers will remain one of the greatest teams in MLB.

All-Stars

The best players from both leagues come together each year for the All-Star Game. This game does not count toward the regular season records. It is simply to celebrate the best players in MLB.

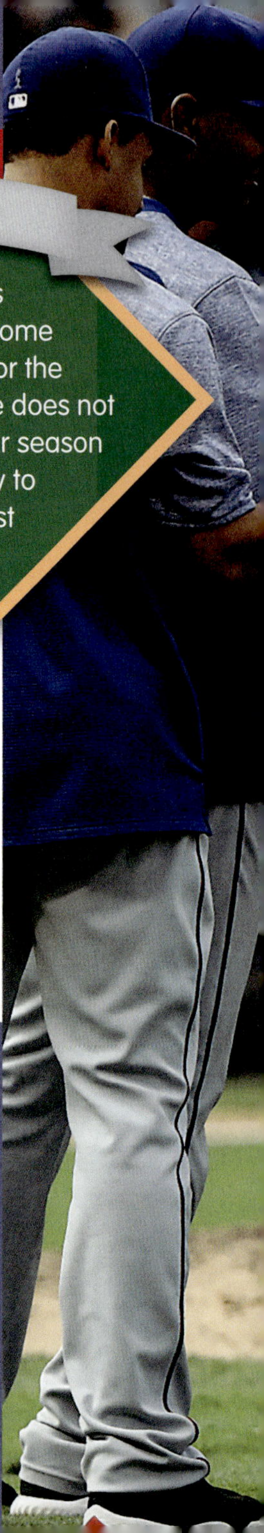

The Rangers finished the 2017 season with 78 wins.

Through the Years

1961

In front of nearly 27,000 fans, President John F. Kennedy threw out the first pitch.

1980

Senator Don Zimmer became the team's eighth manager.

1989

Former President George W. Bush purchased a part of the Rangers team.

1994

The Rangers played their first game at Globe Life Park in Arlington. The team lost to the New York Mets, 10–7.

2004

Four of the Rangers' starting infielders made more than 20 home runs. It marked the second time in MLB history for that to happen.

2010

All-star pitcher Nolan Ryan became president of the Rangers team.

2012

For the first time, nearly 3.5 million fans attended Rangers games in one season.

2017

The new Texas Rangers stadium name was revealed. Globe Life Field will open in 2020.

Glossary

career a period of time spent in a certain job.

champion the winner of a championship, which is a game, a match, or a race held to find a first-place winner.

division a number of teams grouped together in a sport for competitive purposes.

Gold Glove Award annually given to the MLB players with the best fielding experience.

induct to officially introduce someone as a member.

Most Valuable Player (MVP) the player who contributes the most to his or her team's success.

pennant the prize that is awarded to the champions of the two MLB leagues each year.

Platinum Glove Award fans vote for the season's best defensive player who has also won a Gold Glove Award.

playoffs a game or series of games to determine a championship or to break a tie.

postseason a period of time immediately after the regular season. Teams will play against each other in a series of games to find a winner.

professional (pruh-FEHSH-nuhl) working for money rather than only for pleasure.

rookie a player who is new to the major leagues until he meets certain criteria.

run batted in (RBI) a run that is scored as a result of a batter's hit, walk, or stolen base.

Online Resources

Booklinks NONFICTION NETWORK FREE! ONLINE NONFICTION RESOURCES

To learn more about the Texas Rangers, visit **abdobooklinks.com**. These links are routinely monitored and updated to provide the most current information available.

Index